COMMITTED TREASURES

Poems by Anna Jean Felix

By
Anna J. Felix

TEACH Services, Inc.
PUBLISHING
www.TEACHServices.com • (800) 367-1844

World rights reserved. This book or any portion thereof may not be copied or reproduced in any form or manner whatever, except as provided by law, without the written permission of the publisher, except by a reviewer who may quote brief passages in a review.

This book was written to provide truthful information in regard to the subject matter covered. The author assumes full responsibility for the accuracy of all facts and quotations as cited in this book. The opinions expressed in this book are the author's personal views and interpretation of the Bible, Spirit of Prophecy, and/or contemporary authors and do not necessarily reflect those of TEACH Services, Inc.

This book is sold with the understanding that the publisher is not engaged in giving spiritual, legal, medical, or other professional advice. If authoritative advice is needed, the reader should seek the counsel of a competent professional.

Copyright © 2013 TEACH Services, Inc.
ISBN-13: 978-1-4796-0156-1 (Paperback)
ISBN-13: 978-1-4796-0157-8 (ePub)
ISBN-13: 978-1-4796-0158-5 (Kindle / Mobi)
Library of Congress Control Number: 2013932410

Published by

TEACH Services, Inc.
PUBLISHING
www.TEACHServices.com • (800) 367-1844

I express my thanks to God, my family and my friends, who helped to make this book possible.

I would also like to thank the team at TEACH Services, Inc., for their time and patience.

TABLE OF CONTENTS

SECTION I

I See You God 10
God Holds the Power... 12
How Can I Find Him 13
We Come to Worship You.. 14
Nowhere Can I Hide From Thee 15
In the Garden All Alone 16
When I Am Alone With Thee 18
Where Jesus Shed His Blood for Me 19
A Stranger Joined Me 20
God's Love 21
Give of Our Love... 22
What Love Can Do.. 23
See and Feel Your Beauty 24
The Beauty in Everything 25
I Proved You God.. 26
A Quiet Spot to Pray 27
Look For the Good.. 28
Just an Arm's Length 29
He Clasps My Hands 30
Mountain in My Life 31
My Eyes Are Fixed on Jesus... 32
Jesus Be My Pilot.. 33
Jesus is My Shepherd 34
No More Vision No More Dreams................................... 35
No Turning Back... 36
My Only Gift... 38
The Gifts That God Gives.. 39
A Spotless Sky.. 40
The Lilies of Life 41
Free to go From This Cage 42
Love in Action 44
Friendship 45
Walking on the Sandy Shore 46

v

Taking a Walk in Spring Time 47
Music of My Heart 48
My Love for You 49
Here I Vow to be True 50
Is Love a Fantasy? 52
A Place Within My Heart 53
Thanks for My Father 54
Tribute to Mother 55
Let Me be Where Children Are 56
You Will Always Be My Family 57
Longing for His Coming 58

SECTION II

In the Midst of Night 61
The Sky is Not Always Bright 62
The Rain is Coming 63
Thanks for a Sunny Day 64
Soaring Like an Eagle 65
The Journey 66
Love is a Simple Word 67
I Love You Lord 68
My Special Jewel 69
Peasant Girl 70
A True Friend 71
One Special Rose 72
My Mother 74
My Mother's Womb 75
What is Marvelous 76
I Haven't Seen it 77
I Have Felt Your Pain 78
It Is so Still 79
My Last Day 80
Rise Up America 81
A Prayer for Peace in Our Countries 82
Too Young to Die 83
O' Fool 84
Did I Say a Prayer? 85
Forever Gone This Voice 86
Death's Cold Hands 87
Rest in Hope 88

Table of Contents

One Day That Changed America 89
Men and Women of the Law 90
What Prison is Like 91
What Legacy 92
No One Can Take My Home Away 93
This is a Home 94
Thanksgiving Blessings 95
My Heaven on Earth 96
There Are Angels 97
Little Angel Fair 98
My Christmas Gift 99
My Surprise Christmas Gift 100
My Remembrance Garden 101

Committed Treasures

~

Part One

I SEE YOU GOD

I see You God in the lakes and the valleys.
I see Your handprints in the skies.
I see You God in the rainbow above and
The promise You made between You and me.

I see You God in the trees and the flowers,
And beautiful colors, You design them to be.
The birds whistling songs and buzzing bees,
Flying through the atmosphere.

I see You God in thunderous sky and lightning
Sparks flashing through the clouds.
I see You in the tiniest creatures, and
Your mighty powers, so big above,
And I see You God, in the face of a child.

I see the thorns press down on Your brows,
And the blood trailing down Your beautiful face.
Not because it should be, but because of Your love for me.

I see You God nailed on the cross.
Not because You should be,
But You did it all for me.

GOD HOLDS THE POWER

God holds the power of creation, the power of the wind.
He made the mighty ocean, the creatures of the sea.

God's power is so big, and yet so small
I see the big blue whale He made,
And tiny bitty creatures,
Which takes only a microscope to see.

The dolphins in the sea so wise with knowledge too,
a pleasure to behold, the things that they can do.
The seagulls in the air that feed upon their prey,
The tiny creatures in the sea, the fishes all for thee.

God's power is so great, the marvels of this world,
Try figuring it out and see how much you think you can,
Emerging you can see, no matter how we try,
To fathom his mighty power, the deeper and stronger
His powers and the beauty of his love.

HOW CAN I FIND HIM

Oh that I knew where I might find Him;
That I might come to where He lives!
I would order my feet to walk the journey He has taken.
I would know just what the pathway holds for me!

If only I knew what He looks like and the robe
He is wearing now for me.
If only I could see His face and hear Him speak to me!
Would I recognize His voice and understand the words
He'd say to me?
Or turn a deaf ear to His pleading voice?

I see Him in the powers of the storm, the mighty wailing breezes
that blow,
In the sunshine in the eastern sky that gilded the morning dew,
heart beat on arise of day and yet,
I do not know the way He took for me.

I see Him on the cross with pleading words and prayers
That day on Calvary
And yet I do not see the journey He took for me!
I ask the question, how can I find Him?

WE COME TO WORSHIP YOU

On this His Holy day of rest,
We come to worship on God's day,
Which He has sanctified and blessed.

We open now our hearts ajar.
Come in now, Lord, and bless us.
With songs of praise and words of love,
We give you, Lord, our thanks.

May we now worship you today
In spirit and in truth,
Take all we learn today
All through our earthly life
And give to those we meet our given truth of light.
Shine out today, shine out always
Your shining light.

NOWHERE CAN I HIDE FROM THEE

Where can I go and God is not there?
Nowhere can I hide from Thee;
You are the sculptor that formed the world and my very soul.

The peace I feel is the peace of God
That is reaching out to me, and
I am reaching out to Him.

Where can I go, and God is not there?
Nowhere can I hide from Thee.
For the heavens above with its starry sky and moon
Shines at night, look down on me whenever I try to hide.

Where can I go and God is not there?
Nowhere can I hide from Thee.
Go down to the bottomless depth of the sea,
He is right there waiting for me.

IN THE GARDEN ALL ALONE

In Gethsemane for the world, Jesus agonized in the garden
all alone for you and me.
Although His disciples were there with Him,
He suffered in the garden alone.

In the garden alone, Jesus prayed with agonizing pain,
With the cup full for the world, He drank it all alone.
With no one there for Him, He took the cup for the disciples
in the garden
He was alone.

In the garden alone, Jesus asks for help in prayer.
"Watch awhile with me?" He said,
But not even one disciple stayed up to pray with Him.
They fell asleep in slumber, while He agonized on His knees
for them.
How sad for my Savior, Jesus, who came to save this world!

Let's be aware of how He suffered and came to save us all,
Keep our eyes open, be alert in prayer and do good deeds too.
Help Him drink of the cup that was meant for you and me.

In the garden alone,
With swords and staves in hand,
They took Him from the garden
To stand before the common men who were not fit to try
the king,
The king of the most high, Jesus,
Who came to save this world.

In Gethsemane for us, they took Him all alone
To suffer the shame and humiliation.
He was condemned, found guilty, exchanged for a
common criminal,
And He carried His cross to Calvary because of His love for
you and me.

WHEN I AM ALONE WITH THEE

When I am alone with thee my God,
A feeling I cannot express! It is a lovely feeling,
To be with You in prayer.

When I am alone with Thee, my heart beats fast,
I am anxious to express my thoughts to You dear Lord.
I long to tell You how I feel and what I want from You.
Although You know my every need before I even ask!

I am so private and secure when alone with Thee my God.
I tell You the most confidential things,
And know they are safe, no one will ever know,
What we have spoken of.

I love to talk with You each day,
For You lift my burdens all through the day,
And make them light and bright.

You satisfy me with food for thought
And the wisdom of Your words
To carry me all through the day, in a closer walk with thee.

WHERE JESUS SHED HIS BLOOD FOR ME

Step by step I'll walk each day closer to Calvary.
I'll climb to the place where Jesus shed his blood for me.
Where he stood, I'll boldly stand on the hills of Calvary!

I'll take up my cross and follow him,
For he gives me strength each day
to follow him in prayer.

I'll take up my cross and follow him,
For he leads me all the way,
Lifting my faltering spirit
And renewing my courage too.

With my cross I'll watch and wait
Hoping, trusting in the Lord.
With my cross at Calvary,
There's absolutely nothing else to do,
But let him lead me all the way
With my cross to victory.

A STRANGER JOINED ME

I walked along life's lonely road,
In sadness did I walk.
When suddenly a stranger joined me and asked,
"Why are you so sad?"

The reason for my sadness,
They have put my Savior to his death.
I told him how they nailed him on the cross,
The one who is my Jesus has left me here alone.

I told him how others discovered my Savior's empty tomb;
Some claim he is alive, while others argued!
They stole him from the tomb I cried!
Was it necessary that my Savior should suffer and die,
A sinner's death for the world?

The stranger said to me,
How slow to believe and dull of understanding.
Was it not necessary that your Savior should suffer these things?
And enter into his glory?

He told of all the prophets, he interpreted to me
The scriptures the things concerning himself,
His theme was most interesting,
In all the words I heard, of Jesus and His love.

How my heart burned within me,
Then sadness flew from my soul,
For the stranger who walked with me
Was the one about whom this story was told,
I am no longer sad for my savior,
He is risen from the grave and is walking and talking with me.

GOD'S LOVE

When God's love is experienced
In your life, it's easy to share
With others the love he has
Given you.

God's love; It's like a crystal stream
Sailing through its channel
Without any obstacle
Blocking its even flow.

Though the ocean looks treacherous
And the waves are raging high,
There is a calm and peace
When Jesus stands there
Before you.

When God is for you,
Who can be against you?
Though the swift flowing river
Comes upon you,
It shall not overtake you.

GIVE OF OUR LOVE

Give of our love in the time that we have;
    Don't think of tomorrow and the years that we live.
Time is not measured by the fleeing of years,
But by the deeds that we do, and the pleasures we give
    To others as the days come and go.

Let's give each moment and chance that we get,
The love we can share to make others happy in the time
    That we have,and lighten the load of some weary one,
Lost on the road of times fleeting years.

Don't think of tomorrow and the years we may live.
Let's give as we travel this journey in time,
    And think not of years as they pass by.
But give of our best in the life that's spared
For tomorrow may come, and opportunity Lost,
    To give of our love today!

WHAT LOVE CAN DO

Tell me, what can love do?
Capture beauty as beauty should be,
Capture the delicate image and soul,
Capture the love only beauty knows.

Tell me what beauty knows,
Only love the divine love,
The love for us so long ago,
Expressed on a cross no longer stand,
And this love, remains embedded in His hands,
An emblem of His love.

Tell me, what can love do?
Change a life, make it indeed a divinely altered one,
Not a monument of stone,
But of flesh and blood His own Jesus' love,
His precious blood, spilled upon the cross
for you and me,
That's what love can do.

SEE AND FEEL YOUR BEAUTY

Lord, let me see and feel your beauty,
In the harmony and melody,
In creation songs of nature,
Singing birds, and blowing breeze
through the leaves and on the trees.

Beauty in the gardens, on the flowers,
Different species, colors, and green.
Let my heart receive them gladly.
They are your handiwork,
And in these I see your beauty
And the love you gave to all.

Let me see and feel your beauty in your handiwork.
In the sea you made the creatures, and fishes of the ocean.
In your image you made mankind,
to enjoy all of these.
When I think of your love and beauty
And see all of creation,
I know how much you loved us,
you made them all for man.
For beauty is an expression of Your love for us.

THE BEAUTY IN EVERYTHING

Free to see the beauty that is all around us Lord,
When we see it in each other,
    We are seeing God in them.
He made all things beautiful for He is beautiful and good.

God created all around us, man He made in His image,
Not as robots did He make us,
    But as human beings He did.
He made all creatures beautiful, man He made to rule them.

There is beauty all around us
    When we see it through God's love.
There is beauty in the snow cleft mountains,
    The rivers, the lakes, the sea.
There is beauty all around when we see it in the trees,
    The flowers, In the sunshine and the rain,
The springtime breeze, summer, Fall, and winter,
    In each of these we see beauty,
And God in every one.

When we look at God's beauty that is still here to bless us,
We see that He loves us
    And sent His son to guide us
Through this world in which we live.
If we look at His life,
    And follow Him each day,
We see His beauty all around us,
    And in every thing He made.

I PROVED YOU GOD

I chose you God this morning
And proved the holy words
Your light shone through for me,
Although there were some doubts!
That I would see your
Light and come to where it's bright.

I knelt for a moment on my knees in prayer
And listened to your voice
And the light you shone upon me,
Lightend up my life and lifted the burdens and my fear.
Yet in this darkest hour in the depths of my soul,
I cried out for others who need your light,
Dear God.

I chose you God this morning
And proved what you can do.
In just a moment's notice,
You came through for me with understanding Lord!
May I continue, Lord, to listen to your voice.
For you will never leave me in this world of dark despair.

A QUIET SPOT TO PRAY

On the wings of prayer,
I'll fly away from the cares and tensions of life.
I'll close my eyes and let the spirit take part
In leading the words I say.

I know not how to pray Dear Lord,
And what I aught to say.
Just open the door of my heart Dear Lord,
And teach me what to say.
My heart is a temple when you are there.
I invite you now to come in today.
Come in to stay. Come into my heart I pray.

In this quiet place I'll share with you,
A peaceful spot each day,
Where I'll come to meet with you,
In this temple Lord, where I pray.

LOOK FOR THE GOOD

Through the ugly, look for the beautiful
And in the darkness for the light.
Sorrows, crying, sickness, and pain.
In them you see Jesus reaching out
With hands of love.

Look for the good out of all your trials;
Jesus bore them all for you.
Don't despair when they come upon you.
Look up to him. He is smiling down on you.

Keep the faith. He is right there at your side.
Reach out and clasp your hand in His.
Let Him draw you close to Him,
And in His arms be yielding,
More and more your life to Him.

JUST AN ARM'S LENGTH

Just an arm's length away, Dear Lord,
You are waiting across from me.
With your arms outstretched, Dear Savior
You are waiting there for me.

Just an arm's length across from me,
You beckon, "come dear child,
I am waiting right here for you.
Why are you delayed so long to heed your savior's call?
Come to me. I am waiting to hold you in my arms."

"Just an arm's length away I am waiting.
Why can't you see my hands with the nail prints in my palms,
These hands that were nailed on the cross just for you?
Don't you be like doubting Thomas.
Come, have faith, and believe."

HE CLASPS MY HANDS

There are days so dark when I can't see,
    Not even hear His voice,
But my Savior cares for His child,
    So far in distress and dark despair.
He reaches out His hand to mine
    And suppresses my darkest fear.

There are days when I try to walk
    This narrow road before me,
The road I must take, but when
    I'm tired of the toilsome road
Before me walked each day,
    My Friend Divine reaches out His hand
And holds my hand in His.

There are days when I lack the courage
    To put one foot in front of the other,
But then I hear a voice whispering in my ear:
    "I am here to walk with you,
So don't you have to fear."

In the last sad hour when standing alone
    And faith was dim within me,
I felt His hand tightly clasp mine
    There is grace and power in this trying hour,
When He clasps His hand in mine.

MOUNTAIN IN MY LIFE

I'll climb Mount Everest to the top, I know my Lord
Is on the top holding on my safety line.
I know my Lord is holding on my safety line,
I'll place my feet between the crevice steps,
Which I can see between the rocks.

Securely one by one I'll climb, holding on the safety line.
I know my Lord has secured my line
Firmly on the mountaintop.

I climb Mount Everest every day, in life's daily struggles,
Am not afraid of challenges when I know my Lord
Is watching me, Climb this mountain in my life;
He will see me climb it safely,
For He has secured my line firmly on the mountain top.

I'm climbing the mountain in my life for it is very high,
I sometimes reach the point, which is jagged and rough
And make some critical decisions,
Which will determine how safely I climb,
But I know my Lord is at the other end,
I climb Mount Everest to the top.

MY EYES ARE FIXED ON JESUS

My eyes are fixed on Jesus.
I cannot move my eyes, for fear I should fall.
If I can see right through you, Lord,
I imagine what I'll see:
A heart that is so precious, loving, kind, and good,
More precious than the rarest of gems or gold.

My eyes are fixed on Jesus,
I can see how much He loves me.
He knows when I am sad and crying.
When my burdens are too much to bear,
He lifts them from my shoulders, and whisper in my ear:
"Oh, how much I love you, do not feel despair."

My eyes are fixed on Jesus,
I cannot take them off.
If I follow in His footsteps, I will walk where He has walked,
Never slipping nor falling,
If I keep my eyes on Him.

I close my eyes and imagine myself
Walking hand in hand with Him,
Talking, listening, to His voice saying to me:
"You are my child, please don't take your eyes off Me.
Keep your eyes fixed on me…
Even when you are sleeping."

JESUS BE MY PILOT

Jesus Savior be my pilot; navigate this plane for me,
Through the course you have chosen,
    Even when the storms arise.
Navigate this plane of mine,
    Through the clouds around the storms.
In the course You have chosen to its journey's end.

I will fasten my seatbelt, sit back,
And let You hold the steering of this plane.
    Steer me through the course chosen,
With Your chart and compass.
Jesus Savior be my pilot; navigate this plane of mine.

While seated on this plane, let me not be idle,
But keep my mind and eyes focused on the final journey,
    Though the storms are raging,
And it's treacherous and strong.
    I know who holds the steering,
One who says to them, "be still."

Jesus Savior be my pilot; navigate this plane for me.
When at last I reach the journey,
    And the storms are peacefully at rest.
May I hear the words of Jesus say to me,
You have let Me be your pilot.
    And I navigate this plane for you,
To its final journey's end.

JESUS IS MY SHEPHERD

With Jesus as my shepherd,
Why should I be in need of anything?
If I let him lead me in pastures green,
I'll walk with him in peace and love.
He leadeth me besides the still waters,
To drink from the fountain of His life
And never thirst again.

Jesus is my shepherd,
Who makes me whole and pure from sin.
He leaded me in paths of righteousness,
That I may be his sheep, who will stay within His fold,
And never stray again.

Jesus is my shepherd,
Who walks with me through the valley of the shadow of death.
I will fear no evil when He walks beside me.
His rod and staff comfort me and drive away all fear.

Jesus is my shepherd.
Who prepares for me, in the presence of mine enemies.
He anointed my head with oil,
Fills my cup until it overflows with blessings for each day.
I'll let Him be my shepherd to lead me all the way.
His goodness and mercy shall follow me.
If I let Him, be my shepherd He will dwell with me forever.

NO MORE VISIONS, NO MORE DREAMS

In my visions and my dreams,
Let me see in them Your love penetrating all of these.
Let them become reality, not a vision, not a dream
But Your perfect love be seen.

In my vision let me see,
You standing here with me.
In this world's trials, let me be in reality,
Walking here in person with You.

In my dreams I see You Lord.
All that You have gone through for me.
The pains, shame, and humiliation You suffered here for me.

Let me see You Lord, not in visions, not in dreams,
But in reality out of all You have gone through,
see Your joy, peace, and love.
In my daily walk with You.

No more visions, no more dreams.
See You daily in my prayers and songs.
When I hear You call my name,
See beyond the vision and dreams,
A home in heaven prepared for me.

NO TURNING BACK

No turning back to where I have started
For I am following my Savior.
Let nothing or no one turn me around
When I am following just behind the other bend.

No turning back to where I have started
When Jesus is my guide, who is leading on ahead,
Making sure there is nothing in the pathway
So I can safely follow on.

No turning back to where I have started,
For I will lose track of my guide ahead
And be lost with nowhere to turn.
I cannot find the path without the guide to lead the way,
He is the only guide ahead—to lead me on this lonely trail.

No turning back from where I have started.
When I have come thus far ahead.
Turning back will make me lose strength, faith, and courage
To continue on this trail.
With Jesus as my guide, I'll keep pressing on.

I have come this far, to turn right back,
What a failure I would be,
To reach thus far and turn right back to where I have begun
When my Jesus is my guide.
I'll carry on and let Him lead,
For He is the only guide I have to lead me on this trail.

MY ONLY GIFT

My gift I give to Jesus cannot be compared
To the gift He gave me.
He left His Father's mansions and heavenly home for me,
He gave His precious life for a sinful one like me.

My gift I give to Jesus cannot be compared
To the gift He gave to me.
He came to live on this sinful earth
And suffered here for me.

He gives me all his attention; he comforts me
When I am sad and lonely.
Sick and crying, he fed me when I was hungry,
Clothed me when naked and cold.
He gave me all and said to me, "I love you.
Nothing is too much to give you."

My gift I give to Jesus cannot be compared to the way
He suffered for me; He suffered shame of a sinful man
When He was pure from sin, but because of His love for me,
He was stripped from His heavenly raiment and a scarlet
robe was His to wear.
They scourged Him and mocked Him,
A crown of thorns He wore
All because of His love for me, a gift I cannot repay.

My gift I give to Jesus can never be compared
To the gift he gave to me.
In return dear Lord I give you my heart, my life,
That is all I have to give.
You have given me so much more;
I do not know what else to give,
So take the gifts I give to you and lay them up in heaven.

THE GIFTS THAT GOD GIVES

We are so blessed by the gifts that God gives,
So freely for all.
The heavens so blue, loaded with stars,
The rain from above to water the earth
With growth for the plants to sustain us with food.

The flowers of the field, in their endless variety,
Are ministering to us in their beautiful array.
You nourish every root, with hands of care,
To express Your love secure for us.

We are so blessed by the beauty that's here,
In spite of the sin-marred world.
You clothed the field with green,
And behold the flowers with different shades of colors.

Every blade of grass, every opening bud and blossoming flower,
Depict the blessings of our heavenly father
Who gives these gifts to all of us.

A SPOTLESS SKY

One day I'll have a spotless sky,
When all my dreams come true.
    That day will come, and its not far away
When I'll share my dreams with you.

Though far away and I cannot see
If your skies are blue today,
    It matters not, if yours are cloudy,
For my sky is blue enough for two.
If ever you see a cloud appear in the blue,
    Just close your eyes and open your heart
And wish I were there with you,
And your cloud will disappear,
    For I'll be thinking of you

That day will come when my dreams come true,
And my sky will be spotlessly blue,
    When I'll share these days with you
And be held securely in your love.
That day, my sky will be blue again
    And all my dreams will come true.

THE LILIES OF LIFE

How can the lilies be so white
When grown between the marsh and grime,
In ponds of moss and murky waters,
Yet produce qualities so pure?
Without a spot or blemish on their petals,
They are beautiful and white.

Consider the lilies how they grow,
And our lives in this world.
For we, too, can be pure like lilies
Growing in the ponds of sin.
If we let our Savior guide us
Through this world of murky waters,
He can make us just like lilies,
Pure and spotless, white and clean.

FREE TO GO FROM THIS CAGE

Free to go little bird, you are free to go...
I cannot go; this is my home,
This cage you have placed me in.
You gave food, water, sunshine, air
And sometimes opened my cage door.

Free to go little bird—
Did you notice I have opened the door?

I cannot go; this is my home.
I have grown accustomed to this home.
I see the other birds go by.
I hear them sing and sometimes even join their songs.

There is no freedom in this cage.
Stretch out your wings and see,
There's freedom out here for you.
You cannot fly in this cage; there is not enough room to be free.
Come out of this cage,
There's freedom out here for you.
The door is open
Why don't you come out and see?

I'll venture out and see what I can see.
I'm outside of the cage;
The air is fresh, and the space looks vast and wide
I flapped my wings–I noticed I can fly!
There is freedom out here for me.

I am outside of this cage,
I am stretching my wings,
I am flying up and down.
It seems to me, I am freer out here,
But in the cage I was more secure.
My food and water were sure,
But out here I don't know how to survive.

I am outside of the cage.
I'll see how high I can fly.
So I flew up in a tree, perched upon a branch,
And looked down at my cage.
The cage looks small from this distance up here.
How did I make it in that cage,
When up here, I feel so free?

While I was contemplating, a bird flew by and whistled.
I joined him in his chorus, and closer and closer he came to me.
He whispered to me, let's fly away and see what we can see.
There is a vast world around us,
Let's fly away.
Don't look back at that open little cage.

I flew up in the sky, I felt so free.
I am really free. I missed so much when I was in that cage.
Now I fly to other countries, migrate from town to town.
I'm free at last, I am free at last.
No more cage for me.
I cannot see my cage,
That little cage that kept me from freedom.

LOVE IN ACTION

Love is a song expressed through the voice
Echoing music, a symphony and dance.
Love is words expressed through action, deeds,
And simple passion.
Love is being happy for others' actions,
Even when sad, or crying.
Just being together in this situation.
Love is the source of strength.
Love is giving to someone traveling through
Life highway's journey, heat, or storm.
Love is showing someone compassion.
Love is admiring a flower's petal,
Giving to another a rose or a bouquet of flowers.
Love is the source of admiration.
Love is being there for each other
When hearts cleave together, beating fast as one.
Love is unity.
Love is kissing, hugging, excitement of passion.
Love is a miracle of a baby's birth.
Love is the laughter of children playing.
Love is all of these in action.

FRIENDSHIP

Friendship is forever when it is shared with you.
    Your heart and soul are shared,
So bold no one can challenge you.

Each word you speak, each glance
    Expresses friendship so true.
A friend I can depend upon when things are looking grim.

The one who perseveres to bring a smile again,
    A friend I met, not knowing
How the friendship would develop,
    A friend I'll want to keep forever.
And your friendship means the world to me,
    For friends like you are few.

WALKING ON THE SANDY SHORE

Walking on the sandy shore
Watching the rolling waves come ashore,
Slowly through the ocean deep, sweeping onward,
Over sunken treasures in the depth.

Sea-weeds beds beneath them grow, tiny fishes gliding through
In and out they swim and float, not a care, for rolling waves,
Above them roar.

Peacefully they roll, ever thoughtless of the goal.
Ramping, roaring, O! So high, sometimes low with rolling tide,
Crashing on the sunny sand, splash on my wading feet,
Sailing back to gather more.
Taking the same course again pushing on as before,
Catch a glimpse of the distant shore.

O that I might reach the sandy shore, as I journey through The
course, rolling, roaring, pushing by the rocky part,
Side by side the breakers roar, rolling quickly through the pace,
Crashing on the open space, vacant rocks to make a splash,
Sandy shoreline vanish in the heated sand,
Rolling on again once more.

TAKING A WALK IN SPRING TIME

When spring is in the air,
I walk through the countryside
    Taking in all the scenes.
I feel the breeze so fresh and clean,
For winter has gone to bed.
    The sunbeams glitter across the green hills
And the meadows are green with foliage so new,
With growth on trees and flowers of the fields
    With wild daffodils all in a row.

The rivers and lakes flow through its bed,
Beneath the mountains green,
    With colors of flowers so new
Are blooming in the meadows, hills, and dales
As I walk through the edge of the fields.
    I sit on the grass and whistle a tune
Of spring time melody, and the birds in the meadow
Join me in a tune of gladdened view.
    They wing their flight from tree to tree
So graceful; they are free.
I sit on the grass and feel refreshed
    And view the country scene.

THE MUSIC OF MY HEART

Awake my love! Come kiss my lips with tenderness.

And feel the joy of my heart expressed,

Rhythmic songs of melody

And the drumming of my heart

For you.

Come listen to my heart beat

It's beating fast for you.

I hear the thumping sounds it makes.

Beneath the ribcage of my breast are the calling sounds

For you.

Come closer now my love, and lay your head upon my chest,

Closer to my heart and hear the music of the beat.

It's like the drummers sound for you.

The music of my heart.

MY LOVE FOR YOU

I long to show my love for you and let you know just how I feel.
My love for you is so deep, a depth that is within my soul.
Whenever I hear the sound of your voice,
I hear my heart beating, beneath my ribcage, and my breast,
The rhythmic sounds I hear,
Like marching soldiers tramping feet.

My love for you, is like a rainbow distinct with colors
Bowed the skies so pink.
Between the rain and sunshine bright,
My love for you is like the light.

I'll stand up in the storm of night
Until the dawn of day alight,
I'll sail the ocean far and wide,
In high tide, on a wintry night.

The piercing of a dagger's blade,
On a wooden cross I would've laid.
My love for you will feel no ill,
You guide my life Lord, your way, your will.

I long to show my love for you,
Even as I rise above my heavy load,
I'll smooth the wrinkles on your brow
And feel the curves of your smile
I'll hug and kiss you tenderly,
I'll dance, sing, and shout my love for you.

HERE I VOW TO BE TRUE

Rise up my love, my fair one and come away
For the winter is past, the rain is over and gone;
The trees put forth her green, tender leaves,
The flowers appear in the garden and on the trees,

And time of the singing birds has come
Arise my love, my fair one and come away with me
The voice of nature sings; the air is fresh from the winter cold.
The birds sing sweetly in the trees,
And here I vow to be true.

My beloved is gone down into his garden, to the beds of spices,
To feed in the garden and gather lilies.
I am my beloved's, and my beloved is mine;
He feedeth among the lilies in the sweet smells of myrrh.
Thou art beautiful o! my love,
And handsome as a groomed horse, comely as silk,
Terrible as an army marching in a queen's parade.

Don't turn your eyes away from me for they have overcome me:
Your hair is, as velvet thrown around my neck.
Your teeth are as snow flakes freshly fallen upon a green Hedge,
whereof every one is even.

You are my beloved; I have come into your garden
And your lilies are white,
With beds of flowers and sweet smelling myrrh.
Let me sit in your garden and linger here with you.
I am my beloved's, and your desire is toward me.
Let's lodge in the smells for they have overcome me,
And here will I give my love to you.

IS LOVE A FANTASY?

Is love a fantasy? Or it is what I feel for you?
A restless heart that beats so fast whenever I think of you,
A vision in my sleepless nights, a face
I see in my awaking hours, is it a fantasy?

Tell me what I feel and see,
Is it really love for you?
I kiss you in a picture frame,
Say good-night to a recorded tape,
And listen to the message you left me.
When will I stop my fantasy
And come to reality that this was not meant to be?

I go to sleep and dream of you
In a vision I see you uncovered, nude
And cover you with sheets of love.
And yet it was a fantasy!
Awake me from my fantasy,
And make it real for me.

A PLACE WITHIN MY HEART

No time can separate us, when your heart and mine are one.
Though time must pass before I see your hazel eyes,
The intensity, of your smile within my heart,
As memories will restore these in its rightful place.

I'll miss the days you sought me with heart so gentle,
Loving, strong, and true.
A heart that loved and gave so much,
No one can give like you.

And though the days go ticking like a clock.
The memories of yesterday are fresh, the same to me
As though it was that day, you came with a smile and hazel eyes,
Just gazing down on me.
As memories will restore these days a rightful place,
Within my heart for you.

THANKS FOR MY FATHER

Thank you to my Father who art in heaven,
The Creator of Heaven and the earth,
The one who gave to me my father on this earth,
to be my tour guide through life's rugged roads.

I know it was not easy to guide me on this road,
It was rough with boulders and difficult to walk,
But my father looked to Jesus, to guide him
On this road he had to take with me.

When I was just a little child walking with my dad,
I sensed the road was rough to walk alone,
With daddy as my guide,
So I took the hand of Jesus together with my dad's
To walk on life's rugged road with Jesus as our guide.

He taught me how to love the Lord,
And look to him for guidance.
Although sometimes I thought this road
Was very rough for me to walk,
He urged me on with early morning worship,
With songs of praise and prayer, and kept me in the way of
The Lord, to travel this road of life.

And now! I look to Jesus to keep me on this road.
I give You thanks dear Father who art in heaven for the father
You gave to me, who kept me on life rugged road and
Helped me walk with you.
I thank you dad, for the path I am traveling on.
Because you took the hand of Jesus, together with my hand.
I am traveling on life's pathway, together with my Lord.

TRIBUTE TO MOTHER

You were the channel that God used
To bring me into this world,
To carve my mind and character
In the foundation of his love.

You taught me how to respect
The Lord and love His holy word;
You were the example I followed
That kept me close to Him,
I saw you Mother dear,
Sitting day by day on special hours
Studying God's holy words.

You taught me through the things you did,
How to sacrifice and show my love for others.
You went without, made sure I had,
You answered questions that no one else would answer
And steered me in this road I have learned to walk on.

I'm glad you were my mother.
I will not have another,
But only you as my mother.
I miss you so much when you left me on that day,
I thought my life had come to an end
And all my dreams with you were gone forever.

On that day, my heart was shattered!
I had lost my best friend, my Mother,
and had no other friend but my Mother.
I'm glad you were my Mother,
You were the vessel that God used
To bring me into this world,
I will not have another but you as my Mother.

LET ME BE WHERE CHILDREN ARE

I didn't miss the opportunity to be where children are.
It gives me such compassion and makes me really care,
I didn't miss one little bit. My time I spent with them
Was so enriched and full.

I didn't miss the joy, to stop and see what pleasure
I can have, spending quality time with them can bring.
I didn't miss the time to see the creatures great and small,
And have such fun just being a child once more,

I didn't miss their laughter and their songs
And even some cloudy days.
To let them know God cares if they have all of these.

YOU WILL ALWAYS BE MY FAMILY

You will always be my family, even though life bring changes,
And many come and go in generations to come,
You'll always mean the world to me, as my special family.

Now we have come together, to celebrate this festive time,
The reunion of one family and a generation that's now fourth,
We give thee thanks dear Lord for this great big family tree.

You will always be my family, And being close to each of you
Is holding onto the foundation of our home,
And even though our first generation is almost extinct,
We nourish the foundation of our family tree in growth.

By coming here together, let's spread our branches far and wide,
And keep the tree nourished with unity and love,
The main ingredient, for the growth of this family tree of life.

LONGING FOR HIS COMING

I long to see that day,
When pain and sorrow will pass away,
And joy and gladness will come my way.
Lord help me to live with these expectations
That these days are coming soon.

And live each day, in loving, peaceful, harmony
With every one around me,
Waiting for Your coming.
Living in readiness, all dressed in Your righteousness.
Waiting for You to come as Lord of Lords and King of Kings.

Committed Treasures
~
Part Two

IN THE MIDST OF NIGHT

Standing there, in the midst of night,
Looking up into the sky,
One, two, three, four, five, six, and seven,
Trying hard to count the stars,
Winking and blinking as though they were twinkling,
All I got up to was seven.

Then I thought of how God made them,
And in six days He made the earth and heaven.
What a mighty God is He,
To make this earth and all creation
In such a tiny span of time.

Standing in the midst of night
Looking up into the sky,
Thinking of what really happened
And what is beyond this scene,
I would really like to see
And satisfied my curiosity,
But there are circumstances
And requirements to meet,
In order to see beyond this scene.

One, two, three, four, five, six, and seven,
I am trying hard to make it to heaven,
Just to see this marvelous scene.
I'll keep on looking up to heaven,
Until I see beyond this scene.

THE SKY IS NOT ALWAYS BRIGHT

The sky is not always bright with stars,
And moonlight above in heaven's blue dome.
But dark clouds overshadow the stars in the sky
And the moon is eclipsed by
Darkness sometimes.

The sky is bright and lit with stars.
The moon shines bright, illuminating the night
With its light so soft and fair…

Our sky cannot be bright every night,
When shadows of darkness overcast the sky,
And the night is pitch black's darkest night.

The shadows of night that overcast the sky
Are sometimes like our lives,
With moonlit sky and starry heaven above.

THE RAIN IS COMING

The sky is dark; the clouds are thickening, rain is about to fall.
The trees are swaying, the birds are chirping,
People are running to and fro, getting ready for the rain.

I hear the pitter-patter of raindrops on my windowpane,
And see the silver raindrops falling from the sky.
The people are running for cover, the animals too.
But some are walking in the rain; it feels so good to them.

We cannot do without the rain, for it is life to us.
Oh! How the trees look healthier, the grass is greener too.
The flowers are brighter and beautiful with colors.
You can see life expansion through creation and
Even some wilted flowers.

Oh! I love the evening showers; they bring me peace and calm.
Everything is so beautiful after the evening showers.
I love to hear rain falling in the evening and at night,
It gives me such serenity; it gives me peace and rest.
I thank the Lord, the Creator for rain,
Which is water and life to us.

THANKS FOR A SUNNY DAY

Thank You, Lord, for this beautiful day.
For the golden sun that comes up from
The eastern side of the sky,
It takes away the darkness from the night
And lights up my day.

Thank you, Lord, for this beautiful sunny day.
The sun looks like a golden ball placed
Right there in the sky.
Its rays reflect on the dew, wet grass that makes
A picture designed by special hands.

The dew drops sparkle like diamonds,
And glitters between the sun rays on the wet grassy green,
Which makes another design that—
No hands or paintbrush can paint.
This design is special, something only—
The Creator Artist can paint.
On this golden sunny day.

Thank you, Lord, for this beautiful sunny day.
It lights up my spirit,
It gives me peace and joy.
May I pass this on
That they may feel the peace and joy,
It brings to me on this beautiful sunny day.

Thank you, Lord, for this day,
For the sunshine in my soul.
Let it reflect its sunshine to others I see today.
And may they detect its beauty in all I say and do,
For Jesus is the sunshine that brightens up my day.

SOARING LIKE AN EAGLE

Soaring like an eagle high above the world,
With wings outstretched in flight
Floating like air soaring through the atmosphere.
High in the heavens so clear,
I'll fly away and leave this world down here
And build my home up there.

Soaring like an eagle high above the world,
I'll fly to the mountain peak, rest upon its height
And be at peace and rest.
Look around the world below and wish it could be at peace,
No earthly fame or fortune, but make my home up there.

THE JOURNEY

If you could reach the golden stars,
Just climb until you reach them,
Success comes, but with a price:
It's not handed on a platter.

If you could pick the roses in a garden,
They are beautiful to see,
But there are thorns and thistles too
To reach before the rose.

If you must walk this journey,
You must start from one end,
There are circumstances in our goals
And the flag is on the pole.
In order to reach your destined goal,
You must climb the pole.

LOVE IS A SIMPLE WORD

Love is just a simple word.
When taken from the alphabet,
It's spelled with four letters,
And yet it is the strongest word, to build a character.

Just taken slightly, it's a simple word—
That can be used and be abused
In so many different ways.
Love is strong and powerful,
Yet so gentle, so simple,
And so pure a word.

Love can be seen in just a simple gesture.
When you are down and lonely,
It lifts the spirit up
Love can sacrifice itself and not a selfish giver.
Love can keep on being kind even though,
Others envy.

Love does not think of evil,
But rejoices in the truth:
Love bears, believes, hopes, and endures all things.
Love is a simple word,
But greatest of all, love is God.

I LOVE YOU LORD

I love You Lord, for all that You have given me.
Your life You gave on Calvary.
Your precious blood was shed for me.
I love You.

I love You for You set me free,
And I can choose to be.
From all that makes me sin
And really live a life for You.

I love You Lord, because You first loved me,
And now my life is really free,
To love you more each day,
And every day I'll live for You.

I love you Lord. You are my light and my salvation.
You are my very being.
And I am just a wilted flower,
So quicken me, and let me—
Come alive again,
To blossom in this world for You.

MY SPECIAL JEWEL

Daughters are special jewels
God gives to mothers to cherish and keep for Him.
My precious jewel I'll keep for Him,
Securely as my treasure,
I'll cherish her with all I have
My tenderhearted care and love,

I'll make sure she is secure, with precious gifts of tenderness,
And qualities so rare, the ones you have to dig deep for,
The diamonds and the precious gems
My daughter is a special one.

I gave you qualities to share
Of kindness that's sensitive, but rare,
You have the worth of precious gems,
Yet money cannot buy these qualities you share.

My daughter is a thoughtful one,
She shares concerns for everyone,
Her smile so rare, a special one,
And sweet when shared with anyone.
She is my daughter and precious one,
God gave to me my special gem.

My daughter has these qualities,
Now fitted for the world to see,
She is the gem that will shine for them, on this day and year,
And I am the mother standing tall with pride and joy
On this special day,
God's blessings are with you, all through the future years.

PEASANT GIRL

I capture the beauty no one has seen,
in the face of a lonely peasant girl,
Though so sad and cold.

Stricken with the coat of poverty,
I capture the beauty not seen before,
My camera, my finger, and I.
One touch of a button,
And beauty was brought to light.

I capture the beauty hidden there,
Beneath the rugged life.
Oh what beauty, was in her eyes!
Beneath the sad and dirty face,
There was beauty so dignified.

I capture the beauty, beneath the poverty and strife
Behold! What beauty the world hasn't seen before,
In the face of a lonely peasant girl.

A TRUE FRIEND

There is no one like you, a true friend
who I can understand and trust.
To share my hopes and dreams with,
And you'll share your hopes and dreams too
Because you are my friend.

There is no one like a true friend
To share all my joys with,
Sing when I am happy, laugh, and sometimes be very silly,
and you be silly too and laugh right back at me.

There is no one like a true friend
That is very special, when we can spend some time
Just being kids again, to tell all our secrets,
which we will hold most dearly,
and be the friend I have found in you, a true friend at heart.

ONE SPECIAL ROSE

My heart is asking for my sister:
Where did she go?
How did she go?
Where are you, my dear sister?
Are you lying in a grave, or
Walking on some unknown street?

My heart is aching for my sister.
Are you lying sick somewhere?
In a hospital, nursing home,
Somewhere, and cannot tell someone
Who you are, where you are, or
How to find someone you know?

Where are you my dear sister?
I am so very sorry I cannot find you or
Know where you are.
Did you get into an accident somewhere?
Get left on the road to die?
Did someone have compassion on you
And lay you in a secret grave?

My heart is crying for my sister.
Why did you go away like this?
You never said good-bye to me-
You knew I loved you and wanted to be there for you-
All your life you have been there for others
I hope someone was there for you.

My heart will love you forever and
Now I am saying "Good-bye" to you.
I am sorry, my sister, dear
I did not place a rose upon your grave,
Or in your casket, near your heart.
But I am placing one special rose in my heart for you.

Good-bye my dearest sister.
I love what we had together.
My love for you will never fade.
God bless you
And may He mark the spot where you are lying
For He holds the secret of your disappearance.
(For my sister)

MY MOTHER

My Mother is God's chosen treasure
He gave to me this precious gift
To have and hold as a precious treasure,
A gift of diamonds I behold!
She is so rare this treasure hold.

My Mother means so much to me;
She is my heart and soul.
Because of her I have my life,
And she sacrifices all for me.

My Mother is worth far more than the precious gems.
No one can buy her; no one can pay what she's worth.
Yet she has been neglected and treated with contempt—
And shirked she is the rarest gem on earth
And should be treated so.

You cannot buy her character; it's imbedded in her soul.
Love comes naturally and peace is serene,
A noble one to behold.
My Mother speaks with wisdom,
And faithful instruction comes from her.
She is my teacher and my guide.
I'll follow all through my life.

My Mother is so beautiful, a beauty from within;
It comes from her love for God.
She is to be praised; she has earned far more than the rest—
So give her the reward she deserves.

MY MOTHER'S WOMB

In my mothers womb, I am safe and secure,
Tucked in my warm cocoon,
No worries when in here,
Safely in my waterbed, why should I come out for air
When I am safely cuddled in here?

I feel the warmth and I love it in here,
Safely in my mothers womb.
I go where she goes, I work when she works,
And I sleep when she does.
I'm safe and secure in this little space
Why should I come out when all is secure?
I like it in here and I'll stay where it's sure.

Mother, I feel your loving hands smoothly over me,
Making sure of your tender touch,
And daddy's kisses too,
And listening to hear if I am still in here.

I thank you God for loving care, from day one,
You have kept me here.
In this small space you have watch over me—
And see all is well for the nine months,
You have allotted this tiny seed to grow,
Into a baby boy, or girl you know;
But whatever I am, my allotted time has come:

I am ready to come out; my space is outgrown,
and the world is waiting to greet me.
I am ready to see my mummy and daddy and all who await me
In this world I am about to see.

WHAT IS MARVELOUS

It's not what I can see that's marvelous,
It's not what I see before my eyes,
But what I see within my heart,
The marvel of the world
My eyes cannot behold!
I share with others and express
My feelings of joy and inner peace.

Content my heart with gifts of love and what I have,
Though blind my eyes from vision of light
And darkness is the world in which I see.
I live a life with inner "Satisfaction" no light of eyes could
Withhold, for nature with all of its magic,
Makes the darkness disappear
From the peace and contentment in my world.

I HAVEN'T SEEN IT

I haven't seen it, but I have felt it,
Though far the mountains may be.
They're right here each day before me
And I must climb them, daily in my life

I haven't seen it but I have heard the
Thunderous cracking up above,
And lightning flashing through the clouds,
I may not see its flashing light,
Yet I know it's stormy in the skies.

I cannot see the sunlight every day;
It's mixed with stormy winds that blow.
And though sun shines between its glow
I feel the warmth of sunshine,
Through the stormy winds that blow.

I may not see the One who speaks to me,
But I can hear the words His message brings.
With mountains to climb, thunderous skies,
And stormy days, I can still feel the sunshine in my life.

I HAVE FELT YOUR PAIN

When one has gone through pain,
They can feel another's pain,
for they have felt the same.

When one has walked a road,
They can tell how far to go,
For they have traveled on this road
And know just where to turn,
How far before this road
Will come to its traveled end.

If I have felt your pain
And know the length of this road,
How can I not see and feel,
Just what you are going through?
My heart goes out to you,
For I have traveled on this road,
And made the pathway clear for you to travel on.

So travel on, my friend, do not be discouraged;
This road was traveled on before
And is much easier now for you to travel on.
For Jesus traveled on this road—
And is waiting at the end for you,
So, travel on my friend.

IT IS SO STILL

It is so still, death passed by no more your; voice I hear.
It is so still, I listen for your name to call.
In the stillness of the morning hour, why can't I
Hear your voice once more?

In the stillness of the midnight hour the sounds I hear
I am missing only your voice, I cannot hear.
Why did this moment come so soon?
When all was bright and fair for you.

I miss you dear, my precious one,
My lover, and my dearest friend.
I chose you for my life mate and friend;
How dare you break the vows we took?
Until death do us part we said.
I didn't know you'd be the first to part from me the way you did.

I miss your laughter, joys,
And sorrows shared with family and friends.
My love for you will forever linger in my heart.
God's blessings are with you until we meet again.

MY LAST DAY

I didn't know it was my last day: September 11, 2001.
I faced this day as a normal one,
Left my home as usual, said good-bye as I did.
Or left with a curse or swearing,
With a smile or kiss to the ones I love,
Or a prayer on my lips to God above.

I didn't know it was my last.
I took the train, the bus, or drove my car
And maybe walked a block or two to the
World trade towers. I stopped for a bite at the restaurant
Or got there too early, or maybe just a bit too late.

I didn't know it was my last
When the world trade towers were suddenly struck—
By the terrors of selfish men who have no love for humankind.
My thoughts flashed back to my inner soul.
Is it well with Thee, or did I have the time to think,
Is it well with my soul?

It is a day I'll never forget
When America was attacked; they struck the Pentagon too.
The government is under attack.
What pure excitement flooded our way,
A sadness and grief that will never go away
For we have all lost too much.

I didn't know it was my last.
So be careful how you live each day.
Pay attention to what you say and do.
Keep a prayer on your lips as you travel life's way.
For you never know when your last day will come.

RISE UP AMERICA

Rise up America, rise up, stand tall again.
Don't let these falling towers crush your city's pride
But raise up towers, tower once again.

Rise up America, you are a towering power! Stand tall again,
Wave high your banner stars and stripes, march on to victory
March on.

Rise up America, rise! In unity and brotherly love.
Don't let it take disaster to bring us close together
Realizing we are one family, a family of God united as one.
March on in peace and love.

Rise up America, stand tall, stand firm again.
Brave men and women fell, with your towers tall and strong
In a city that we love and a country brave and free.

A PRAYER FOR PEACE IN OUR COUNTRIES

Pray for peace on earth in a world where war
And rumors of wars abound, and terrorism is a daily fear
For millions of us around,
We need to pray for peace and love
More than ever in these days.

Pray for peace among all nations, color, creed, and race,
The sadness and the terror that encounter us in war,
The lost property, the wealth, the fame, the fortune,
And most of all, the loss of human life.

Pray for the war in our lives of selfishness and greed,
The hate and hardness of our hearts,
The lack of love for others.
How can we be the children of one Father,
The Creator of this world, when hate is so intense
Among our brothers and us sisters?

Pray for peace in our souls, and our wars will cease,
Wars in our lives, wars in this world, and we shall live in peace,
In a world of relief where love shall reign and never cease.

I long for that place where there will be no war,
Where our Saviour is Jesus, who can bring us
To a home where the angels soar.

TOO YOUNG TO DIE

What causes us to have love for others
And want to risk our lives?
Because we have the love of God and know
That God himself is love.
Why should we let disaster show how
Important communication is to us,
When some are hurting secretly
And it's always dark for them?
Let's learn to shine our torch of love
And light the part they travel on.
For life is traveled in the dark,
A lonely road for some.
You stood there with the pistol,
Loaded with the steel,
And emptied it one by one
In a class of innocent ones,
Who had nowhere to run.
They died there,
Some heroes;
Yet too young to die.

O' FOOL

Where art thou o' beauty,
whose glory had been the pride of all,
Had been cut down in the
Vigor of your youth?
A memorial marked your grave
Was the blood spotted pavement.

Why go to that extent
To prove your strength
And power, when you are
Just one breath in flight
And passing through
So swiftly?

DID I SAY A PRAYER?

Did I say a prayer when I went to bed that night?
Did I have a dream or a vision?
Or was I still asleep and not awake at all?
Am I still dreaming that this dreadful day has come?

Did I say a prayer before I left my room
And thank God for His blessings?
What a beautiful morning!

Did I call my mum or dad or someone else I love
To say how much I care?
Or did I leave my room in an angry mood
And didn't really care?

Did I take the time to think of what am doing here
Or lend a helping hand to someone in my path?
Did I leave them lying there
Or rise up when the opportunity arose
And give a helping hand
Before it's too late
To turn back the time?

FOREVER GONE THIS VOICE

I hope its not forever, your voice is gone in death
But when Jesus comes again, I will recognize it yet.
I hope it's not in vain, you have lived here on this earth
But gone to sleep for a little while,
Until Jesus calls your name.

I cannot hear your voice,
I listen in the wind,
In the stillness of the day, the night,
In the people running by,
But I cannot recognize your voice.

I hope it's just this sleep in rest,
And not a sleep of death.
When Jesus calls your name you will answer,
"Here am I dear Lord, I have waited for you here.
I am ready to go home to live with you
Forever and eternally with you."

DEATH'S COLD HANDS

When death cold hands caress me, and I shall let it lift me,
To the heights eternally I'll stand, this mortal clay will die,
And wait for God to quicken me, and eternally I'll rise.

Eternal heights I'll stand no more to see corruption,
For my God is eternal.
This earth will be transformed
And sunshine will rise, eternally will shine,
No more to see the darkness,
This death that earth suppresses—
But rise eternally to stand.

No sin or corruption nor sadness or crying, only love forevermore
I'll live for that eternal life when God shall make me immortal,
And I shall live forevermore with him.

REST IN HOPE

I long now to rest in the depth of the earth,
In a tomb for my bed, and peacefully rest,
When the Life Giver calls, I will answer
Because I am not really dead, but waiting for him.

I long for the rest that will lighten my load,
Unless I am waiting to be transformed with my Lord,
One thing is certain and that is our death.

But when waiting in the hope that he is coming again,
I die with assurance he is coming soon.
My friends and loved ones with him we'll ever reign.

ONE DAY THAT CHANGED AMERICA

One day, the day that changed America; September 11, 2001,
People going to work, in a day of sunshine bright and fair,
Not knowing what lay ahead, went to duties assigned to them
In life, their work's chosen call.

One day that changed America, for better or for worse,
A day when terrorists struck, and we all ran amok.
Which brought us all to one accord, in love and harmony.
They came with helping hearts and hands to give of all we had.

One day when people came together, all around the world.
A day we showed a broken heart and love filled one and all.
A day I cried for those I knew, and those I didn't know.
A day we came together, it took this day to show,
How much we care, and love each other.

A day that changed America, a day we'll never forget,
When love was shown for all people, creed, and race.
Although our towers fell, our pentagon destroyed,
Our comrades lay wounded and dying,
May we with towers stand tall again, united one and all.

MEN AND WOMEN OF THE LAW

Men and women of the law,
You are heroes; you are brave.
Men of uniform, women of courage,
Standing for the freedom and morality of the law.

You are called to duty, dangerous and fierce
Sometimes when at home in bed,
With family all around tucked in for the night.
The phone rings with the call that message brings.
Not knowing where the danger lies,
You are up and running to answer the call.

As men and women called to serve
Speed with urgency from the caller's voice
Are on the roads and highways.
No matter who, where, or when,
You are faced with the dangers of your life in your hands.

Called to duty, you have pledged
To uphold the law and see it kept.
You will protect the streets, both night and day
To see our citizens do their part,
To uphold the law that was given by God.

The call came on September 11, 2001
When all in uniform rushed to the scene
To rescue those in dire need.
You climbed in the dark of the smoking towers
to rescue strangers in those dire hours.
You didn't know them, no not one, but duty calls and you obey.
It is a pledge you have made,
In life or death you must serve.

WHAT PRISON IS LIKE

I wonder what prison is like.
Imagine dark, lonely, sad, and cold.
A quiet that is beyond peace, frightening
A dark that is beyond darkness and pitch black's darkest night,
That empties the soul of joy, peace, and happiness

If only we can open the prison doors of our heart wide, wide,
So Jesus can see inside and come in every corner of our cell,
Remove the sadness, the loneliness, and depression
That blocks our door from opening
And enlighten it with joy, peace, and hope
That one day soon, there will be no more prison.

To enter a prison, it has to be a choice we have made
To choose to disobey the law
And stand the consequences it brings,
To be shackled in handcuffs and chains,
Then placed within a cell, with bars upon our window gate

Oh Lord! Let me be free, I want to be free, I feel like screaming
Lord, let me be free, from this choice I have made,
Oh! Make me open this prison gate.
Come in dear Lord, I invite you in this prison cell of my heart,
Set me free: I have made the choice. I want to be free,
Oh! Let me be free from the prison cell I have chosen.

WHAT LEGACY

What legacy was handed down, what legacy my life portrayed,
The life I live would surely tell when I am no more in this life.

What legacy I leave behind, my life lived on earth,
Would demonstrate,
Should it be one portrayed, in a monument with famous names?
Or written on a dungeon cell,
The life lived here would surely tell,
What legacy I'll leave behind.

The memories of stories told,
Of men or women whose names the world refuses to call
And tell the stories of their worthless lives,
Their lives here should reveal it all.

What legacy I should leave behind,
the one that I would like to tell,
in a written record of my life I'll share,
in books and stories with famous ones.

What legacy was handed down the one I'll like the
youth to know and pattern their lives by my legacy, and
leave their prints in famous paints,
and not the blood from human veins!

NO ONE CAN TAKE MY HOME AWAY

No one can take my home away.
No one can build this home for me.
All earthly things will come and go,
But the home I want, no hands on earth can build for me.
No one on earth can buy this home;
The master builder will build for me.

The one I want to live within, the structure is strong.
No storms can toss nor billows wash away.
It's beautiful with lighting of His natural glory,
That shines brighter than the sun.
It is tinted and gilded with beauty.
Landscaped with varied scenery,
And designed by the Master Artist.
A floral Eden garden, with exotic heavenly beauty,
No one has seen before.

No one can take this home away.
It's designed by the Artist, who called it into view.
This surpassing beauty scene is in heaven.
Where He is building this mansion for me,
And it's there my home will be.

THIS IS A HOME

This is a home and not a house.
A home is a place where God is the head
And every one sings His praises every day.

A home to teach our children respect and love for others,
A home I'll come to, when not secure outside,
A haven and a shelter to protect us
From the danger lurking out there.

A home where Jesus is our welcomed guest,
Seated at our table in time for every meal.
Where prayer is heard at breakfast, at midday,
At dinner, and just before our bedtime.

A home where Jesus is consulted when things are hard to solve.
He is the one who knows and solved them all for us.

THANKSGIVING BLESSINGS

For in giving you receive,
And your blessings God freely gives,
Baskets full of thanksgiving goodness
   Open now your heart to receive.

He will give what you ask for when he sees it's what you need,
Not a stone will he give you,
When you ask of him for bread.
Now give thanks for daily blessings,
And creation which he made,
Of this world, and heavenly beauty
God's sustaining love bestows.

Be a messenger for Jesus, cheering the sad,
In times of trials making them glad,
He who loveth gives all to guide us—
   Blessing all that betides.
Do something for somebody every day;
Help them along life's heavenly way.
Jesus the example to follow, scattering blessings to all we meet.
And give thee thanks for all these blessings,
And our daily life received.
The breath we breathe is not our own,
And for this we give God thanks.
For the sun shining beauty, and this day, we have received,
Now thank God for these blessings,
And in return we'll give thee our hearts.

MY HEAVEN ON EARTH

Right here upon this earth, where my angel lives with me.
I want to make it heaven where You and I, can live each day
Within the haven I make.

Where You can live in peace with me,
And teach me how to live in love,
And exercise each day the love you gave to me.

I want my heaven to be a place where you can rest a while,
From toiling daily here with me, and listen to my songs and praises,
The stories of the day.

I want my heaven to be a place where friends and family
Can come to stay.
And meet with Jesus every day.
And live for heaven above.

THERE ARE ANGELS

I know that angels are with us all the day.
But, we cannot always see them,
Only in some special ways.
There are good ones
And there are bad ones, who disobey God's law.
The good ones are His servants, who minister to our needs.
God gives us angels, everyone,
To guide us in His way.

I know angels are special, for I saw them in my prayer.
One day when I was praying and in meditation on my knees,
I saw a hole up in the sky, with a bright light shining through,
And the reflection of that light was coming down on me.
I saw so many angels on both sides of that light,
I knew God had sent them to minister to me.

Angels are special, godly beings who come to our every need.
God sends them to protect us and help where needed.
He sends them in the form of people
Who will do some kind deed, or remove obstacles
Blocking our pathway.

If only you come to Jesus,
You will see them in His life.
For angels walked with Jesus when He lived on this earth.
And when we walk with Him,
There are angels walking beside us.
So let us walk with Jesus,
In prayer and good deeds too.
We will have our Savior and His angels
Walk with us each day.

LITTLE ANGEL FAIR

He is an angel come to earth, a little angel
Born from birth, his life down here is very tough
But he held on although so rough.

Angel, angel, come to earth, from the moment of your birth,
You were summoned to come for the purpose you serve here
Your courage strong and faith endures, you little angel dear.

Little angel, your songs will sing on and on in our hearts
As you sing sweet songs for us
From the songs of your heart.

Little angel fair,
You were offered anything this world could afford to give
But, what you chose to have instead
Were gifts of prayers from God above.

MY CHRISTMAS GIFT

No one can buy my Christmas gift;
No one can sell this Christmas gift.
It just cannot be bought.

No one can pay the price it's worth;
It's far more than the priceless treasures of this earth.

No one can buy this gift for me.
It's given free to all,
Not a gift for me alone,
But all who will receive it.
This precious gift is Jesus Christ.

MY SURPRISE CHRISTMAS GIFT

My Christmas surprise is not shopping
In the wintry month of December
When the stores are decked with lights—
And all good things to buy
In colors red, gold, and green.

The stores and streets are lit with décor,
And songs echo the Handel Christmas Carols,
Reflecting Christmas time is here.
The people bustle through the streets,
Towns, cities, shops, and stores,
Hustling, buying, and dressing homes
With lights and fancy ornaments
Hanging on Christmas trees,
In special corners of the house with bows, wreaths,
And trimmings hanging from the ceiling
Makes a special flare.

The home smells of baking and cinnamon in the air,
Apples, grapes, and pears with a citrus cluster
In a centerpiece right there.
The bells and whistling songs ring,
And Christmas Day is here.

The trees dressed with glittered hanging ornaments,
And gifts tied up with ribbons and bows,
In bags of different kinds.
And this Christmas morning shines.
Gathered around the tree, all were ready to receive,
But the most important gift of all
Was missing from under this tree.
The one God gave to me was not tied
With fancy ribbons and bows,
But wrapped in swaddling cloth in a manger far away.
The surprise gift for me was missing beneath my tree.

MY REMEMBRANCE GARDEN

Let me leave a legacy of my life implanted in a garden,
With colors rare, indelible, printed on someone's heart
to see, a legacy to follow.

A garden you can walk in, when you are sad and lonely,
A garden you can linger in, when your joys are overflowing, And
troubles come your way, a Gethsemane garden,
Where you can kneel and pray and see the flowers bloom again,
A legacy garden.

Let me leave a legacy that shines in the dark,
A lighted torch to carry on, and light up someone's part,
A legacy with memories to remember my life.
I want to leave a garden, full of precious gifts of love.

What legacy was handed down, what legacy was left behind,
My life lived here would surely tell,
A patterned life of Jesus, the one that He has lived.
And this! The one I'll leave behind,
In my remembrance garden.

We invite you to view the complete
selection of titles we publish at:

www.TEACHServices.com

Scan with your mobile
device to go directly
to our website.

Please write or email us your praises, reactions, or
thoughts about this or any other book we publish at:

P.O. Box 954
Ringgold, GA 30736

info@TEACHServices.com

TEACH Services, Inc., titles may be purchased in bulk for
educational, business, fund-raising, or sales promotional use.
For information, please e-mail:

BulkSales@TEACHServices.com

Finally, if you are interested in seeing
your own book in print, please contact us at

publishing@TEACHServices.com

We would be happy to review your manuscript for free.

www.ingramcontent.com/pod-product-compliance
Lightning Source LLC
Chambersburg PA
CBHW041614220426
43670CB00001B/18